Pennies
From Heaven

Molly Schaar Idle

Abingdon Press

Nashville

Pennies From Heaven

Scripture quotation is from the New Revised Standard Version of the Bible.
Copyright © 1989 by the Division of Christian Education of the National Council of Churches of Christ in the U.S.A.
Used by permission.

Scripture quotation identified as NIV is from the HOLY BIBLE, NEW INTERNATIONAL VERSION.
Copyright © 1973, 1978, 1984 by International Bible Society.
Used by permission of Zondervan Publishing House. All rights reserved.

ISBN 0-687-49505-9

06 07 08 09 10 11 12 13 14 15—10 9 8 7 6 5 4 3 2 1

Printed in China

For Alexis, Dawn, and Erika –
there through thick and thin.

Trust in the LORD, and do good.
Psalm 37:3

The world is full of WHYs.

Why is the sky blue?

Why does the grass grow?

Why do I have my mother's nose...

Why does two plus two
equal four?

One "Why" that gets asked
quite a lot is:

Why do bad things happen?

And that is a very good question.
Of all of the "Whys" that have ever
been asked, it's definitely right up
near the top of the list.

293. WHY DO CATS ALWAYS
LAND ON THEIR FEET?

294. WHY DOESN'T ANY-
THING RHYME WITH
ORANGE?

295. WHY DOES THE
OCEAN ROAR?

296. WHY?

297. WHY?

WHY?
1. WHY DO BAD THINGS HAPPEN?
2. WHY DO I HAVE TO EAT MY PEAS?
3. WHY CAN'T I STAY UP LATE?
4. WHY DO BIRDS FLY?
5. WHY DO THINGS FALL DOWN AND NOT UP?
6. WHY NOT?
7. WHY DID THE CHICKEN CROSS THE ROAD?
8. WHY IS WATER WET?
9. WHY IS THE SQUARE
OF THE HYPOTENUSE
TO THE SUM OF THE
THE REMAINING SIDES?
97. WHY DO FEET STINK?
98. WHY DO WE GROW OLD?
99. WHY DOES "I" COME BEFORE "E" EXCEPT AFTER "C"?
100. WHY DOES E=MC²?
101. WHY AM I ME AND NOT YOU?
102. WHY IS GRASS GREEN
103. WHY IS THE SKY BLUE?
104. WHY DID DINOSAURS DISAPPEAR?
105. WHY DOES THE MOON
173. WHY ME?
174. WHY DO BIRDS SUDDENLY APPEAR, EVERY TIME YOU ARE NEAR?
175. WHY

There is no question that some genuinely stinky things can happen in this world. Just look at the morning news and see!

But the world is also spilling over
with goodness!

How can this be?

The fact is, we're positively
surrounded by blessings –
but you have to know where to look.

You see...

Good and bad are two sides of the same coin.

Like work...

and play!

Wet...

and dry.

Up···

and down.

Night...

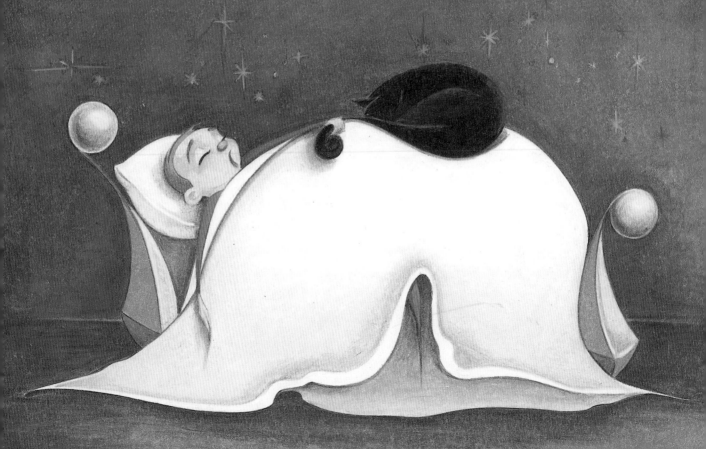

and day.

Heads...

and tails.

You can't have one
without the other.

So, the next time life puts
something unexpected in
your path, don't be afraid.

**Pick it up and look at
both sides of your
penny from heaven...**

You'll find the good.
(In God We Trust.)

The End

Hold on to the good.
1 Thessalonians 5:21 NIV